IN CARVOEIRO

Also by Peter Oram

Poetry

WHITE and other poems

TEASE IT FREE

Novels

MADDOCKS

THE RUB

Translated poetry

From the French-language poetry of R.M. Rilke:

VALAISIAN QUATRAINS

ORCHARDS

ROSES

From Russian:

THE PAGE AND THE FIRE

Contributing translator to

THE PENGUIN BOOK OF RUSSIAN VERSE

PETER ORAM

IN CARVOEIRO
AND OTHER SEQUENCES

SPM Publications
Unit 136, 113-115 George Lane, South Woodford,
London E18 1AB, United Kingdom

www.spmpublications.com
www.sentinelwriting.com

First published in Great Britain by SPM Publications – an imprint of Sentinel Writing & Publishing Company Limited in December 2015.

Cover painting *Self-portrait with mask* (acrylic on canvas) by Peter Oram Copyright © 2015

ISBN 978-0-9935035-1-1

Contents

PREFACE

Just in case you were wondering, none of the poems in the cycle *In Carvoeiro* are translations from the Portuguese any more than are the much better sonnets of Elizabeth Barrett-Browning, from whom I stole the subtitle. They just happen to have been written during a few weeks on the Algarve early in 2015.

None of the poems in the collection have been previously published. As for the question of why three of the four sequences are in sonnet form, it is probably because that form is a kind of infectious disease and has to run its course. I think that after this lot I'm gradually getting over it and I hope that the final sequence (the title of which is also irrelevant, or at least, as they say in title deeds, "for purposes of identification only"), is a step in the right direction.

Peter Oram
Schwabach
December 2015

1

IN CARVOEIRO

(OTHER SONNETS FROM THE PORTUGUESE)

IN CARVOEIRO

(OTHER SONNETS FROM THE PORTUGUESE)

1.

Waking to a parallelogram
of light. Top left, and maiden queen of this
immaculate domain the thin white whisper
of a crescent moon. A single palm,
that's opened like a fan and silhouetted
against a wash of pale celestial blue;
third, from left to right, in yellow hue,
a railing running, like the long and fretted
neck of some exotic instrument
that no one noticed, no one ever played.
It seems a world that time forgot to visit
until a careless brush begins to paint
a cloud or vapour trail, and the exquisite
moment goes, the magic starts to fade.

2.

The moment goes, its magic starts to fade
as soon as you become aware of it.
The moment in the future's mobile, fluid.
The present hardens, crystalizes it.
The moment in the future's like a candle,
perfect, virgin, waiting for ignition.
The present moment's both the match that kindles
and the puff that is the flame's perdition.
The present is the future's *raison d'être*
though simultaneous its birth and death,
but sharply focussed thought or the romantic
heart can somehow make it infinite.
It may approach you quiet as a breath,
or roar in like a storm from the Atlantic.

-

3.

Last night a storm roared in off the Atlantic,
each time it woke me more intense again,
ripping at the stubborn night with frantic
talons, hammering the window pane
like an apocalyptic beast. Secure
and warm beneath the sheet and coverlet,
a secret's length away from me you draw,
exhale, then draw again the gentle breath
of sleep. Outside the morning's grey parade
comes creeping in. The hurricane has fled.
another dawn: decisions must be made.
Whether to go my fumbling, stumbling way,
and step into the lonely damaged day,
or slide back in beside you in the bed?

4.

I slide back in beside you in the bed.
draw in the gentle warmth your form creates,
a potion that both reinvigorates
and calms. It's several hours since daylight fled.
The quarter moon completes its quiet arc
towards the ocean through the starlit sky,
a seabird that I can't identify
performs its cool cantata in the dark.
The body isn't difficult to please:
its simple hungerings are swiftly sated;
the soul's more subtle, seeks its satisfactions
in illusions: these the higher self may seize
and cleanse, thus love is differentiated
from just one more of those cliché attractions.

5.

Though now it's just one more cliché attraction
there's beauty here that cannot be denied —
the way it's balanced high above the tide
that with its slow, relentless grinding action
will one day send it crashing to the sea,
the way the little chapel's perfect, white-
washed walls hurl back the brilliant solar light
as if it mocked its own mortality.
I walk the golden beach for one or two
of those appointed hours that I'm still due,
along the line between this little land
and endless ocean, whose almighty mill
will never cease to grind and grind until
the last shell, bone or pebble's turned to sand.

6.

The last shell, bone or pebble turns to sand.
The great machine of time slows down and ceases
turning. God, the charioteer, releases
the reins, the ship of fate sails in to land.
The people go about their daily business,
drink their coffee, read their magazines,
take their daily pills and eat their greens,
content to leave the world the way it is.
The year grows old and bonfire night is nearing.
Several million pounds go up in smoke.
But who cares anyway, there's always plenty
more to come. A woman waits in searing
heat for water, doesn't get the joke.
A cruel wind blows down on São Vicente.

7.

I sing this for the winds of São Vicente
where the eye feeds on infinity
and hungry gannets gather in their plenty
then drop like silver bullets in the sea.
I saw the winter sun: it went down fighting
against a cloudbank. Though it lost the fight,
before it died its blade broke through, igniting
the entire sky with incandescent light.
Night lays its leaden shroud upon the Cape
of São Vicente: blacker now than blood
the darkness thickens all across the West,
sets all things living longing for a sleep
that would be endless, dreamless if it could.
The winds of São Vicente never rest.

8.

The winds of São Vicente never rest.
There's always turmoil on the borderline
between two different worlds, and yours and mine
are no exception; as with east and west,
or day and night, or continent and ocean,
the frontier is the place of fitfulness,
and of fertility and action, it's the place
of blazing sunsets, battlefield commotion
of lovers both in quarrel and in kiss.
There's an avenue that leads across the green
wide fields of noon, and there's a path that runs
meandering through the meadows of the moon,
some may choose, but all I know is this:
I have no choice. I walk the line between.

9.

All afternoon I walk the line between
where water touches and where water doesn't
touch. Although the weather's fine there isn't
a soul in sight. I zip my coat up, lean
into the wind, my heels crunch the sands—
the cast-off debris of the ocean's fauna.
Returning, later, I decline the sauna,
and settle for the gentle press of hands.
She's twenty, pretty, thus even the dreadful
piped music may not bother me that much—
may even help to clear away this headful
of meandering thoughts. Before she starts,
she heats sweet-scented oils. There are some parts
she touches and some parts she doesn't touch.

10.

Some she touches, some she doesn't touch
and those she touches cannot be quite sure
if she'll return again as often or
at all. She used to make me laugh so much
and then she'd change my laughter into words
which she'd transform to little birds and then
she'd turn them back to laughter once again
—or into different words or different birds.
But recently there's been a change, she's quietened
down a lot, she rarely smiles. I'd said
I wanted to pursue the deeper ways
among the shadows. This, perhaps, had frightened
her. I should have come less close. Instead
I broke her distance. That's the price you pay.

11.

Sudden waking. There's a price to pay
for oversleeping, for it's almost eight.
The night has gone, the ashes of the day
before lie grey and chilly in the grate.
The curtain opens on another morning,
another act of slowly changing scenes:
you've found yourself without a moment's warning
on roundabouts of regular routines.
Too soon I see you turning on the pillow,
too loud the water splashing in the shower.
The lion paces, restless, in his cage.
The minutes fly, they chase the wasted hours.
the sunlight paints its bright and taunting yellow
on walls and windows, on the empty page.

12.

On walls and windows, on the empty page,
strange marks or symbols starting to appear,
fading in, now clear, now not so clear,
like portents from some other, vanished age.
Obscure, then momentarily familiar,
hints of Hebrew, Arabic, Chinese,
or Hindustani—yet they're none of these,
though undecodable they seem to fill your
entire being with a quiet foreboding,
you feel as if you're breaking at the seams
until—it's like a little bomb exploding—
you see they're nothing less and nothing more
than those few words you wrote the day before
fragmented by the rocky ride of dreams.

13.

Fragmented by the rocky ride of dreams,
those uninvited guests of restless night,
the mind rebels, gets ready for a fight
and challenges the will that has not quite
awoken yet, mocks all those firm decisions,
all those early-morning-resolutions
as vain, unnecessary and a nuisance.
It's clear now that a head to head collision
is coming. But the will's not yet defeated—
it's stubborn too, and summons up the soul.
The rebel now observes itself outnumbered,
is swiftly brought back under their control,
concedes defeat and, free and unencumbered,
gets down to work until the job's completed.

14.

Get down to it until the job's completed?
If that were all there was to do in life,
it wouldn't be too hard, but with a wife,
a job, the washing-up still piled foetid
in the sink, two hours spent in heated
arguments about the price of beef
or whether one should fly to Tenerife,
or dentist-visits for those long untreated
fillings, all those chores you keep forgetting
to fix that rooftile that's forever letting
in water, pay that bill so long unsent …
to be a poet—how much harder than
to be an average woman, average man—
why all this ranting on? It's evident!

15.

The woman's ranting on—she's evidently
off her rocker—first in Portuguese
then, spotting me, she slips with perfect ease
into a garbled English. To my gentle
comment there immediately ensues
a flood of unrepeatable expletives,
then she's silent. On her bony shoeless feet
she goes. But who's this dapper dresser who's
appeared without a sound behind my back?
Who's courteously offering me assistance?
What he actually is offering is crack,
Moroccan red, and crystal, Paki black …
Is this regression to some old existence,
or have I strayed way off the beaten track?

16.

I must have wandered off the beaten track,
got lost among the winding country lanes.
This often seems to happen when the brain's
on overload. I'd reached a cul de sac,
could not go forward, nor could I select
reverse nor find a place where I could turn.
But lately I have just begun to learn
that if I'm still and patient I'll detect
that wooden stairway, old, with shaky sections
that descends through cliffs and brambles and
emerges on a perfect golden strand
extending endlessly from left to right
and where the sea's ablaze with blinding light
and fishing boats rest snug on their reflections.

17.

Sailboats resting snug on their reflections.
Those masterminds of espionage, the terns,
absorbed entirely in their own concerns,
cruise the waterline in both directions.
Not far from me a little boy is tossing
pebbles at a ring scratched in the sand.
His aim is accurate and steady and
his eye is cold. He'll make a good assassin.
The sky above's a faultless, cloudless blue,
blue as the cloth of silk laid over you
before they close the lid and nail it down.
But let's not talk of things like that right now.
The waiter's coming over anyhow.
The shuttlebus is waiting in the town.

18.

The shuttlebus is waiting in the town
to take the people back to the hotels
for cocktails on the terrace, evening meals,
buffet selections big enough to drown
the lot of them. There's Connie from Carmarthen;
several grey old ladies small as elves;
that cycling pair from somewhere way up north, thin
and gaunt, almost, as handlebars themselves;
there's Jackie, ever cheerfully depressive;
a New Zealander who's always on his own;
Tom, eighty-three years old and still obsessively
flirtatious. Yellow sun on yellow stone.
East and West are at it once again
chucking bombs about in the Ukraine.

19.

They're chucking bombs about in the Ukraine.
decapitating tourists in Iraq,
and suddenly a balaclava (black)'s
the only fashion extra to remain
an option. On the Algarve all is quiet.
All the hotel guests are on the beach.
Alone up here, you've all you need in reach.
British Rail's on strike. Parisians riot.
With summer there will come the great invasion:
this coast will almost sink into the sea.
You watch the crowds in your imagination
Raid beaches, shops and supermarket shelves
while you sit here and wonder wistfully
whether problems ever solve themselves.

20

Can the problems of the world resolve
themselves or are they only solved by action?
Is entropy the offspring of inaction
or can the world somehow renew itself
through bold and innate creativity—
the kind of force that can invent a rose,
a Beethoven, a butterfly? Through gross
neglect, malicious action we
have brought our planet to the state it's in:
the thread that holds the hanging sword is thin
and growing ever thinner by the day.
The only way to win is this: we must
combine stupendous will with stubborn trust—
time flies: the future's almost yesterday.

21

Time passes quickly: only a few days
to go and we'll be gone; meanwhile, we're high
up in the Serra de Monchique where I
sit waiting while you park. A thick blue haze
hangs over the Algarve's coast, has hidden
the architectural extravaganzas
of the expats, while up here, like dancers,
old and arthritic, caught all of a sudden
in awkwardly arrested poses, cork-
oaks lurk among the pine trees and the eu-
calyptus. At another table near
to mine, absorbed completely in his work,
a man taps at his lap-top. "Hey—are you
a writer too?" I call. He doesn't even hear.

22

Are you a writer too? If so you may
have heard that little voice that keeps on calling,
often incoherent, like the crawling
of insects on dry paper, or the tinny greyish
crackling of an untuned radio.
Sometimes it's gone for days, perhaps for weeks,
and it may shock you when at last it speaks
to you again without a warning. Though
there are those times when you could almost hate it,
and long for it to be eliminated
(for what it wants of you is so immense),
its intermittent, quintessential words
can let you fly as freely as the birds
and make your life full, vibrant and intense.

23

What makes our life so vibrant and intense
is moments when—not often by intent,
more often by some curious accident
or else with some divine or karmic sense
of which we're ignorant—it comes in touch
with other lives so different from ours
yet drawn to ours by some magnetic force
that orchestrates their unmatched tones in such
a way that blends them in the most astounding
harmony. I walked the sands and found
Jorge and Marco, golfers by profession.
At sunset, the arcane initiation:
Jorge whacks golfballs far into the sea:
their dazzling arc is purest poetry.

24

That dazzling art that we call poetry
has dumped of late a little of its dazzle,
become a bacon bit burnt to a frazzle,
a Cinderella no one wants to see.
The best and biggest bookshops barely stock it—
not worth it … not for only four or five
copies a year ... but why, then, in my pocket
this embryo that's struggling to survive,
this crumpled till receipt or shopping list
with hasty lines of scribble on the back?
In the beginning was the word—which one?
Is it still ringing? Does it still exist?
These are the codes I idly try to crack
while sitting at my table in the sun.

25

Sitting out with Jackie in the sun
and waiting for the coffee to arrive,
not doing very much, just being alive
the old and simple way with none
of all those extras that society
often demands. Even the disco music
dribbling from the speakers endlessly
doesn't disturb, is just another neutral
component of the current local scene.
There have been so many times thus wasted.
How will they tally in the final score?
Are they what they are and nothing more
or might they be the moments when we've tasted
The eternal—places where the gods have been?

2

POETRY BY NUMBERS

POETRY BY NUMBERS

ONE

A single bottle, out of reach,
half empty, on the topmost shelf,
a radio left upon a beach
conversing softly with itself,
the prisoner dying in his cell,
the clown who weeps beneath his mask,
Orpheus when the gates of hell
fell shut, the fool who failed to ask
the question in the citadel,
the last one living on the earth,
the empty bucket in the well,
the tiny baby at its birth,
the last leaf left upon the tree …

—the curse of singularity.

TWO

You and I: a solar system
just a single planet travelling
round a pale and lonely sun
slowly, endlessly unravelling
itself among a million million
other stars that turn and twist, a
microscopic dot set in
its own space-time continuum.
Destiny, design or chance?
Who knows—we cannot ever quite
be certain whose those forces are
that set us in this dreadful dance

or say which one if us is star
and which of us is satellite.

THREE

Three of a kind. Upon the heath
they meet and speak and part again.
Above, the grey and drizzling rain,
the damp and spongy earth beneath.
The first will watch the children throwing
coloured balls up to the sun.
The second holds the mirror showing
all the deeds already done;
he loads them in a haversack
which then is shouldered by the third.
Though this weighs heavy on his back

he sets off, joyful and alone
to flounder in the great unknown
in search of the unspoken word.

FOUR

I hung upon a wooden cross
and saw the thieves to either side
saw how they bled, heard how they cried
in rage and agony, because
somewhere inside themselves they knew
that both of them were doomed, were fated
to be snuffed out, obliterated,
whilst I would rise as good as new
as if by magic three days later.
And so I said, by way of trying

to comfort these poor, wretched sods
that they, too, soon would sit on God's
right hand if they'd be patient, wait a
bit. However, I was lying ...

FIVE

I am a secret no one knows
and nobody can understand
my lines are carved into your hand
secured by perfume of the rose
and padlocked by a pentagram
to which there is a single key—
the apple plucked from Eden's tree.
I cannot tell you who I am,
and yet you know me, so it seems,

for I've been roaming through your dreams,
—and I've been lingering in the hush
of moments when you ceased to rush
and poisoning, like some strange disease
the oceans of your memories.

SIX

In later years, though, I have felt
increasingly a sense of home.
September sun is slowly melting
honey in the honeycomb,
and cherry trees are all aflame,
the autumn wind is soft and warm—
and yet, this darkness in the air ...
It's not of nimbus—it's the swarm

of bees who suddenly, en masse
have risen, transferred their allegiance
in a shameless act of crass,
unprecedented treason to
a different queen, some parvenue
who'll wrench them off to other regions.

SEVEN

The pattern of the Pleiades
is echoed in the little jewel
I gave you at the funeral
of all our dark intimacies.
Oh how could it evaporate,
the liquid silence of our love,
leave nothing but the sparkle of

its crystalline precipitate?
The moon mutated seven times.
I found another field to plough,
I found another seed to sow
I reaped the harvest of my rhymes,
but somewhere in the night I know,
unseen, it glistens, even now.

EIGHT

You held me in your eightfold arms
I felt your fingers digging in:
the indentations in my skin
will never go away. What harms
me more though is the way your net
has drawn its threads around my heart

that's now unable to impart
to blood its former forward fret.
I stagger through the barren plains,
the empty pitcher in my hand,
go pouring out its nothingness
upon the dry and hostile land,
the sun marauding, merciless,
the blood stagnating in my veins.

NINE

Though he now lives the last of lives
allotted him he is content,
no longer cares if he survives
in constellated firmament
or not, indeed perhaps he's glad

that he's accepted now that twelve's
enough, and there's no need to add
one of his other several selves.
He'll never roam the roofs again:
he, once the wildest of them all's
become spectator at the ball
where damsels dance and lords are leaping;
he's tired, awaits the moment when
the lights go out and he'll be sleeping.

TEN

See! He descends the rocky slopes,
he wipes his brow, removes his shades.
Behind him on the mountain tops
the lightshow slowly pales and fades.

It seems he's been away for ages,
seems they've forgotten he's the boss
for down below the party rages,
naked women dance and toss
their newborn babies in the flames
and men fall shrieking on their knees
before the golden effigies.
His brother greets him sheepishly.
He passes him the DVD
then leaves them to their lurid games.

ELEVEN

Last-minute shoppers crowd the streets
lured by lascivious store displays
thus Zeus used his divine deceits

to lure Himalia and place
her firmly in the family way.
On the mighty walls of Tescos
giant fluorescent frescos
show us Santa in his sleigh
and on the corner next to Boots
eleven pipers play the last
nowell upon their plastic flutes.
It's clear to us that Christmas now's
the festival of Mickey Mouse.
The beggars kneel. We stagger past.

TWELVE

They sit around the narrow table,
look at him with hungry eyes.

They're still uncertain whether they be-
lieve his dizzy strategies.
Outside in the sable night
the constellations come and go,
engrave their never-ending flight
in the ecliptic, like a slow
unfolding row of sequenced tones
from whose relentless, fixed parade
there's no escape, no retrograde.
He'd call his father, but his phone's
kaputt, the battery's dead.
He pours the wine. He breaks the bread.

THIRTEEN

Condemned from birth, I'm spare. Unwanted.

Tautological. Despised.
The one you thought you'd exorcised
but who each time returned and haunted
your house and home, your heart and mind.
You branded me. You called me beast.
You flung me from the wedding feast.
But I crept in again behind
a mask, put poison on the spindle.
I am the wind that courses through
the darkest, secret parts of you
confirming all your private fears
and though you sleep a thousand years
you'll never kill the flames I kindle.

POSTSCRIPTUM

FOURTEEN

Come live with me and be my love
and leave me when you've had enough.
Love me tender love me true
or it's me who'll be leaving you.
Be my funny valentine:
everything you own is mine,
some things that I own are yours
but not the bank account of course.
You are the sunshine of my life,
that's why I chose you for my wife
and though so far I'm not complaining
I'll run like hell if it starts raining.
True to each other till we die
and if you cheat then so will I.

TWENTYONE

The cards are stacked. They've faked the deal.
You cannot win, but all the same
you know you have to play the game,
this personal *Glasperlenspiel*
assigned to you before your birth
whose complex rules you'll never know—
are aces high or aces low
or both? Or neither? How on earth
to make decisions—stick or twist
or slip a card behind the wrist?
Come! Now's no time to give up hope!
It's either break the bank or bust.
Insha'Allah! In God we trust!
Down we go! Up periscope!

THIRTYFIVE

Somewhere, *nel mezzo del cammin'*
di nostra vita, I went through
a sticky patch, when things came to
a head. For many years I'd been
adrift and buzzing like a blue-
arsed fly—chaotic, wasting time,
till, fumbling, stumbling in the dark,
I lost my vision, had no spark—
Directionless, with neither rhyme
nor reason in the things I did.
But now things built up to a head
until the monster I'd created
imploded, shattered, detonated.
The debris settled: I was flying
in clear skies, blue, electrifying.

ONE HUNDRED

When he smashed through the barrier he
must have been doing at least a ton—
a flash of black, an engine's scream,
a cloud of dust and he was gone.
A couple of miles after Swansea,
spotted by a squad car which
gave chase, he threw the stolen Harley
Davidson into a ditch.
Some weeks later he was caught. He
gave them lip, they gave him hell.
I still can see him, although forty
years have passed or maybe more,
helpless, crumpled, in his cell,
sobbing his heart out on the floor.

3

IN FLIGHT

3

IN FLIGHT

1

It's going to be a bumpy flight, with gales
of eighty over Amsterdam, and worse
to come, it's certain, by the time we cross
the English Channel and fly into Wales.
Eventually this giant cocktail shaker
will dump us on the tarmac and reload
while I pick up the hire car, take the road
out west, while wondering: will it really make a
difference to you anyway that I
have dropped all those so-called essential tasks,
have left a note for anyone who asks
where I have gone, have packed a bag and flown
back through the years and miles, cold and alone
to be beside you, watch you as you die?

2

It's going to be a bumpy flight, with gales
eighty over Amsterdam. This one-
year-old who's perching in the row in front
of me's already had enough: he yells
and yells; no matter what his parents try—
the cuddle or the cootchikoo, the bounce,
the prod or grin or tickle—there's no chance:
there is no way that they can pacify
the flailing child. While fumbling for a pen
I feel the Hohner cross-harp in my pocket:
I draw it out and breathe a note or two,
pianissimo. There's sudden stillness. Then
a face appears, mouth round, round-eyed. The shocked
amazement lasts till landing time is due.

3

Storms west, and wondering, will it make a difference
whether I get on that connecting flight
or miss it and get put up for the night
as compensation for the inconvenience ...
For minor changes in a schedule may
like grains of sand in wheels of great machines
that over time grind all to smithereens,
wreak utter havoc in your destiny.
The woman in the bar that lonely evening,
the stranger who invites you to a show
are like a kind of karmic leavening
that swells the present out of all proportion:
you cast aside all common sense and caution,
cast off all that you value, love or know.

4

Eight-thirty into Amsterdam. What's worse
is, my connecting-flight's already gone
and surely there's no place more dismal than
an airport on your own at night. But first
things first. I slowly make my way to gate
A23 where, sorry for myself
I buy from a confectionary shelf
outrageously expensive chocolate.
I sit down. On the seats across from me
with bony faces wizened by the sun
a timid pair who say they're from Peru.
They take the offered truffles cautiously.
Do you believe in God? He asks. I won-
der if I'm lying when I say I do.

5

Meanwhile, before the giant cocktail shaker
can lift us up and dump us down in Wales
we follow arrows to a sign that tells
us: passport check. It seems it's going to take a
while to get through this, for up ahead
some dumb official's stubbornly berating
a frail old lady. Helpless, hesitating,
she wipes a tear away and shakes her head:
it's clear she doesn't even get the gist
of this whole sad interrogation session.
Stranded, far from home, racked by depression,
she slightly overstayed her leaving date.
For him she's an Al Zheimer-terrorist.
I shuffle forward, offer to translate.

6

Two comets, certainly, before they cross
each other's path, cross half eternity
and who could grasp the endless filigree
of those exquisite patterns that they trace
in doing so. Our life's a line between
two points, it's true—but what a line! Its leaping
and plunging spiral's so complex that keeping
abreast of it's impossible. A keen
observer though may note its echoings
in the fingerprint, that little token
of our individualities,
may recognize in nature's patternings
in sunflowers or in seashells, re-awoken,
the dancing of a billion destinies.

7

The English Channel! Onward into Wales!
The world turns slowly back beneath the plane,
bears with it lives I'll never live again,
the stamping grounds, the old hitch-hiking trails,
those starting-points where we took off from town
the M4, Hammersmith, the Old Kent Road,
the screech of brakes, the moment when we'd load
our rucksacks in. A truck might take us down
the road a couple of miles where we'd be stuck
for hours, but there were days, too, when with luck
a Cadillac would stop, a voice would say,
"Where? Paris? Sure—I'll take you all the way!"
—and everywhere those friends who welcomed us
like watering-holes within the wilderness ...

*8

Well, damp as Sunday dharma country load…
I'd fallen fast asleep while on the plane
and woke with this strange phrase still on the brain.
Was it some kind of esoteric code
or was it piffle? In my sleep it seemed
a message from my long-forgotten youth
a particle of fundamental truth,
of all the trivial dreams I'd ever dreamed
the single jewel that I dared not forget.
And yes—I woke, remembered it, and yet
though it in dreams made sense it now made none.
Now every day and everywhere I go
it rings within me, insolent and slow
and inaccessible—*Well, damp as Sun …,*

9

As I pick up the hire-car, take the road
out West, I feel my mind and body racing
and yet a sense of opening out, embracing
this land, this world, the whole tremendous load
of creatures it contains, a sense of holding
my past, my future, all that lies therein,
in perfect poise, as balanced on a pin—
a sudden sense of endlessness unfolding,
on, outwards from this point of stillness on
this little bridge that is my present life,
of holding all for whom I suffered love—
mother, father, lover, friend or wife—
in one love-ocean independent of
this body that will rot when I am gone.

10

I've gone, I've gone, I've packed my bags and flown
out with the eagle to the edge of time
where the earth surrenders to the ocean
and creatures still converse in one same prime
and universal tongue that nowadays
is never heard in any earthly nation
for none could bear the truth that it conveys
and only certain species of cetacean
might still respond to certain turns of phrase.
Its syntax is the spiral of a sunflower,
its grammar is the flutter of a wing.
With seven words for *you* but none for *I*
it's barely possible to speak in anger
and utterly impossible to lie.

11

It's different for you, isn't it, the way that
your life's gone, when looked at next to mine,
but what's life anyway? It's just a line
between two points, if we'd define it at
its purest level. Up a step however
and moving from a static image to
a more dynamic one, then one must view
it as trajectory, the arrow's ever-
onward flight from bowstring to the patient,
waiting target. I would rather, though,
step sideways, see it as a garden that
will start out simply as a dark and loamy
soil. How it turns out will depend on
what kinds of weeds or flowers you plant in it.

12

You dropped all those so-called essential tasks,
you threw away your list of things-to-do,
you locked the doors, you pulled the windows to,
you latched them, filled a pair of thermos flasks
with lukewarm tea and in the dead of night
you tiptoed past the still half-sleeping watch
and, tightening your belt another notch,
you passed out through the gate and out of sight.
The one who lies in coal-dark rooms, who's waiting
with silver tongue and poisonous green eyes
has tuned your frail heart to the pulsating
ground-bass of the pounding passacaglia
of (*calando*) your descent into the valley. A
pianissimo last chord. The music dies.

13

She'd left a note for any who might ask
where she had gone and pinned it to the door,
filled the harvest of her life into a basket,
and took the way she'd never gone before.
Her body was less heavy now, and soon light
as feathers were her feet upon the ground;
she passed along the alleys in the moonlight,
waking no one, for she didn't make a sound.
At the waterside the ferryman was waiting
in the shadows, but he never breathed a word.
She shivered as she stood there hesitating,
then turned to give a final glance behind,
cleared the last few thoughts out of her mind
and, cautiously decisive, climbed on board.

14

Back through the years and miles, cold and alone
and to a playground in the drizzling rain ...
hands still hot and smarting from the cane
for things he didn't even know he'd done
a six-year-old stares out between the railings
at the inaccessible outside,
shivering, knowing even if he cried
they'd only add it to his list of failings.
Meanwhile behind him, whirling, screeching, screaming
the rest are Spitfires, Stukas, Messerschmitts:
he doesn't turn to watch them playing lest
they gun him down. The bell rings, and the teeming
crowd absorbs him, yet already it's
quite clear to him he's different from the rest.

15

To be beside you, watch you slowly dying,
to be the witness of your final breath,
those final hours of hurting, twisting, crying
before your soft transition into death ...
to see your thin white arms outstretching, reaching
so desperate for the help that none could give ...
your eyes, so dark and hollow and beseeching,
still fighting, hungry with the will to live ...
your face at last so yellow, pale, unreal, with
its final and complete tranquillity,
a life, a light, a world beyond recall ...
... but what will now remain a part of me
as long as I still have a heart to feel with
is the horror and the beauty of it all ...

16

It's going to be a bumpy flight, with gales
of eighty over Amsterdam, and worse
to come, it's certain, by the time we cross
the English Channel and fly into Wales.
Eventually this giant cocktail shaker
will dump us on the tarmac and reload
while I pick up the hire car, take the road
out West, while wondering, will it really make a
difference to you anyway that I
have dropped all those so-called essential tasks,
have left a note for anyone who asks
where I have gone, have packed a bag and flown
back through the years and miles, cold and alone,
to be beside you, and to watch you die.

4

SIX PREMATURE EJACULATIONS

SIX PREMATURE EJACULATIONS

I

the rain in the bed and the
pool downstairs,
the cackle of jackdaws

in green silk,
the unicorn's whistle in the deep bells
early morning

where the planets rise
over bleak telephones
we had it once

you and I

but the milk turned

and zebras fell from the heavens

and it was not enough

            now your hard hands

grasp

at the long and silver water

and it passes between your fingers

and through the straw cushions and

the silent holes in ashtrays

II

greek sunsets over the
wince of lemons
and something hard and pointed and blue

how did you dare to go across
rubbing your shoulders on brambles
and the curve of nightingales?

why did you open the door
and close it again
on a basketful of bitter dreams?

you are the colossus of rhodes

astride the wide sea passages

crushing the dry temples of the wind

with your doc martens

and screaming at the stars

in the street

men with clown masks

paint swastikas on the walls of churches and brothels

and a child clutches at the long grass of the orchard

and cries

II

there are three of them

they appear in a beam of bright light

unfasten their cases

and take out their thin apparatus

that will take you by the scruff of your suffering

and hurl you

into the soft bed of the infinite

they turn and twist

and a fine sand dances upon the skin of the drum

they turn to look at you

and you know you are the Christ

hanging on the cross-hairs

of their telescopic sights

the thieves got off with a caution after all

and

you are alone

IV

wax traffic wardens with hyphens on their sleeves

wait in front of the windows

of banks and supermarkets

they are the priests of impatience

and the custodians of the disabled

and of unaccompanied females

by midday they will have melted

as swiftly as the wings of icarus

yet they will discover an extended existence

in the plastic tape barriers at road accidents

in the livery of the hornet

and in the threefold amulet

of radioactivity

V

why do you grip me again between

your lips of steel?

I am your direct and indirect object

the accusative to your nominative

and you are my mole grip

my araldite

my vise president

I met you in the appendix

to a large dictionary

where I was digging for a lost syllable

that had something to do with culpability

while the children sat at the breakfast table

blowing bubbles in the ablative

the seagulls have returned from the refuse mounds

and the back entrances of hotels

and have assembled in crowds

on the lowtide sandbanks

of the estuary

laughing like metaphors

VI

This is number six
and then the dog will wake up
and want his master's voice

meanwhile he is rotating slowly as usual
on his gramophone of dreams
his ear to the great horn

why do you sleep so soundly?
is there a molecule of morphine
in the bitter almond

that rests under your tongue?
or is the sound of the six-four chord
not enough

to break you out

into the cadenza of your day? ...

am I but a semiquaver

to your mighty breve?

is it not time

we saw the fable of hare and tortoise

as an esoteric pointer to the solution

to the riddle of time?

should my wakefulness wake you

come into my arms and sleep

and wake again ...

and sleep

... and wake and sleep ...